FARM ANIMALS

# Sheep

Jared Siemens

www.av2books.com

Go to **www.av2books.com**, and enter this book's unique code.

**BOOK CODE**

**AVT86477**

**AV² by Weigl** brings you media enhanced books that support active learning.

AV² provides enriched content that supplements and complements this book. Weigl's AV² books strive to create inspired learning and engage young minds in a total learning experience.

# Your AV² Media Enhanced books come alive with...

**Audio**
Listen to sections of the book read aloud.

**Video**
Watch informative video clips.

**Embedded Weblinks**
Gain additional information for research.

**Try This!**
Complete activities and hands-on experiments.

**Key Words**
Study vocabulary, and complete a matching word activity.

**Quizzes**
Test your knowledge.

**Slide Show**
View images and captions, and prepare a presentation.

**... and much, much more!**

Published by AV² by Weigl
350 5th Avenue, 59th Floor New York, NY 10118
Website: www.av2books.com

Library of Congress Cataloging-in-Publication Data

Names: Siemens, Jared, author.
Title: Sheep / Jared Siemens.
Description: New York, NY : Published by AV² by Weigl, 2020. | Series: Farm animals | Includes index.
Identifiers: LCCN 2018049915 (print) | LCCN 2018051579 (ebook) | ISBN 9781489695307 (Multi User ebook) | ISBN 9781489695314 (Single User ebook)
  | ISBN 9781489695284 (hardcover : alk. paper) | ISBN 9781489695291 (softcover : alk. paper)
Subjects: LCSH: Sheep--Juvenile literature.
Classification: LCC SF375.2 (ebook) | LCC SF375.2 .S54 2018 (print) | DDC 636.3--dc23
LC record available at https://lccn.loc.gov/2018049915

Printed in Guangzhou, China
1 2 3 4 5 6 7 8 9 0  22 21 20 19 18

122018
102918

Art Director: Terry Paulhus   Project Coordinator: Jared Siemens

Weigl acknowledges Getty Images, iStock, Shutterstock, and Alamy as the primary image suppliers for this title.

**FARM ANIMALS**

# Sheep

In this book you will learn

how they look

what they do

what they eat

why we keep them

and much more!

3

# Sheep

A sheep is a farm animal with a thick coat of fur.

Farmers keep sheep for food and wool.

Texas has more sheep than any other state.

A baby sheep is called a lamb.

Lambs weigh between 5 and 8 pounds at birth.

A lamb can stand 90 minutes after it is born.

Sheep have two toes
on each of their four feet.

Their feet are called hoofs.

A sheep's fur is called wool.

People use sheep wool
to make clothing.

One sheep can make
up to **30 pounds**
of wool in a year.

Male sheep are
called rams.

Some rams have
curled horns
on their heads.

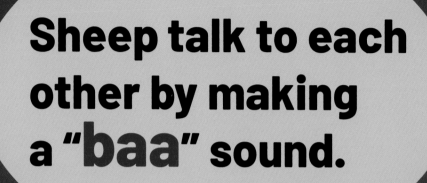

Sheep talk to each other by making a **"baa"** sound.

The noise sheep make is called bleating.

# Sheep eat mostly grass and other plants.

Sheep do not have top front teeth.

Sheep live in groups
called flocks.

A flock of sheep moves together from one place to another.

Sheep farmers often have special dogs.

Some dogs keep sheep safe.
Other dogs guide them home.

# SHEEP FACTS

These pages provide detailed information that expands on the interesting facts found in the book. They are intended to be used by adults as a learning support to help young readers round out their knowledge of each unique animal featured in the *Farm Animals* series and why it is kept and raised on farms.

**Pages 4–5**

**A sheep is a farm animal with a thick coat of fur.** There are more than 70,000 sheep farms and ranches in the United States. As of November, 2018, the country was home to about 5.21 million sheep. Texas, California, and Colorado have some of the largest sheep and lamb populations in the United States. Texas farms are home to nearly 750,000 sheep.

**Pages 6–7**

**A baby sheep is called a lamb.** A female sheep, or ewe, will give birth to as many as three lambs in a single litter. Lambs are born with thick fur called fleece. A lamb can walk within a few hours of being born. Lambs will often sleep up to 12 hours a day.

**Pages 8–9**

**Sheep have two toes on each of their four feet.** Hoofs are thick, hard, and similar to bone. Sheep hoofs are cloven, or divided into two toes. They give sheep steady footing when they walk through uneven grass and mud. When a sheep is in danger, it can run faster than an Olympic sprinter.

**Pages 10–11**

**A sheep's fur is called wool.** Wool is soft, light, and warm, making it perfect to use for clothing. People use sheep's wool to make many things, including sweaters, scarves, and socks. When farmers shear, or cut off, a sheep's fleece, it does not hurt the sheep. A single sheep fleece could be spun into a 123-mile (200-kilometer) long strand.

**Pages
12–13**

**Male sheep are called rams.** Rams in some species of sheep have large, curled horns on their heads. They sometimes use their horns when butting heads in competition with other rams. The Suffolk is the largest sheep breed in the United States. A mature Suffolk ram can weigh up to 400 pounds (181 kilograms).

**Pages
14–15**

**Sheep talk to one another by making a "baa" sound.** Sheep bleat to communicate how they are feeling. Although they are usually quiet, sheep will bleat if they need to get another sheep's attention. Sheep will also bleat when they are hungry, or about to eat. A lamb can recognize its mother by the sound of her bleat.

**Pages
16–17**

**Sheep eat mostly grass and other plants.** A sheep's top lip is split in two. This makes eating plants easier. They can use their lips like fingers to grab a leaf from a bush and pull it off. A sheep uses its bottom teeth to grind food against the hard roof of its mouth. Like cows, sheep spit up their food and chew it a second time.

**Pages
18–19**

**Sheep live in groups called flocks.** Flocks of sheep can have as many as 50 sheep. Sheep will develop close friendships with other sheep in their flock and will often be seen grazing with the same group. President Woodrow Wilson used a flock of sheep to keep the White House lawn trimmed during World War I.

**Pages
20–21**

**Sheep farmers often have special dogs.** Herding dogs, such as border collies, are used to guide sheep in and out of fields and barns on the farm. A herding dog will run around and bark to guide the sheep into groups. Guard dogs, such as Maremma sheepdogs, are kept to protect sheep from predators. They may bark to help scare away an animal that is threatening the sheep. Farmers may also keep donkeys, llamas, or alpacas to protect their sheep.

23

# KEY WORDS

Research has shown that as much as 65 percent of all written material published in English is made up of 300 words. These 300 words cannot be taught using pictures or learned by sounding them out. They must be recognized by sight. This book contains 58 common sight words to help young readers improve their reading fluency and comprehension. This book also teaches young readers several important content words, such as proper nouns. These words are paired with pictures to aid in learning and improve understanding.

| Page | Sight Words First Appearance |
|---|---|
| 5 | a, and, animal, any, farm, food, for, has, is, keep, more, of, other, state, than, with |
| 7 | after, at, between, can, it |
| 8 | each, feet, four, have, on, their, two |
| 9 | are |
| 10 | in, make, one, people, to, up, use, year |
| 12 | heads, some |
| 14 | by, sound, talk, the |
| 17 | do, eat, not, plants |
| 18 | groups, live |
| 19 | another, from, moves, place, together |
| 20 | help, home, often, them |

| Page | Content Words First Appearance |
|---|---|
| 5 | coat, farmers, fur, sheep, Texas, wool |
| 7 | lamb, minutes, pounds |
| 8 | toes |
| 9 | hoofs |
| 10 | clothing |
| 12 | horns, rams |
| 14 | bleating, noise |
| 17 | grass, teeth |
| 18 | flocks |
| 20 | dogs |

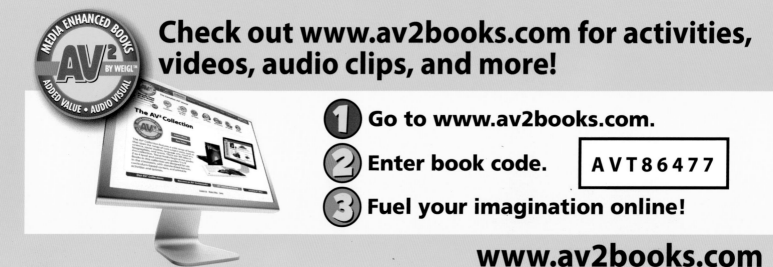

## Check out www.av2books.com for activities, videos, audio clips, and more!

**1** Go to www.av2books.com.

**2** Enter book code.  AVT86477

**3** Fuel your imagination online!

**www.av2books.com**